CONTENTS

MIGHTY TRUCKS

Trucks are the mightiest machines on the road. Trucks carry all sorts of cargo, from parcels to petrol, but they also put out fires, lift loads, fight battles and mix concrete.

TYPES OF TRUCK

Trucks do dozens of different jobs for us, but there are only two main types of truck. They are articulated trucks and rigid trucks (see below). An articulated truck is made up of a tractor unit and a semi-trailer. The semi-trailer carries the cargo.

Trailer attachment
Also called the 'fifth wheel'

Sleeping compartment
Contains a bunk and washbasin

Cab
Contains driving controls

Engine compartment
Contains engine and other parts

An articulated truck. Behind the cab is a sleeping compartment for the driver.

4

Mighty
TRUCKS

CHRIS OXLADE

W
FRANKLIN WATTS
LONDON • SYDNEY

An Appleseed Editions book

First published in 2006 by Franklin Watts

Paperback edition 2008

Franklin Watts
338 Euston Road, London NW1 3BH

Franklin Watts Australia
Level 17/207 Kent St, Sydney, NSW 2000

© 2006 Appleseed Editions

Appleseed Editions Ltd
Well House, Friars Hill, Guestling, East Sussex TN35 4ET

Created by Q2A Creative
Editor: Chester Fisher
Designer: Mini Dhawan
Picture Researchers: Simmi Sikka, Somnath Bhowmick

ISBN 978 0 7496 7589 9

Dewey Classification: 629.224

A CIP catalogue for this book is available from the British Library.

Picture credits
t=top b=bottom c=centre l=left r=right
Aam Alberti: 21t, Amdac-Carmichael Limited: 20t, American LaFrance: 20b, Atkins-Racing: 25t, Daimler Chrysler: 6t, 11b,
Elgin Sweeper Company - A subsidiary of Federal Signal Corporation: 12t, Fassi Group: 17b, Ford: 22b, Freight Liner:
Cover, Fuso Truck and Bus Corporation: 28c, General Motors: 22t, 29t, Jason Ellis: 25b, Kenworth Truck Company, a
Division of PACCAR: 4b, 9b, Liebherr Minning Equipment Co.: 26b, Mack Trucks, Inc: 11t, 14t,
Oshkosh Truck Corporation: 12b, 13t, 18t, 19t, 29b, Scania Trucks: 4t, 5b, 7t, 7b, 9t, 15b, 31t,
Sterling Trucks: 21b, Steve Huddy: 8b, Tadano Faun: 16b, 17t,
Volvo: 6b, 10b, Wecar Trucks and Technology: 19b, Western Star Trucks: 27b,
www.travel-images.com: 27t.

Printed in Singapore

Franklin Watts is a division of Hachette Children's Books

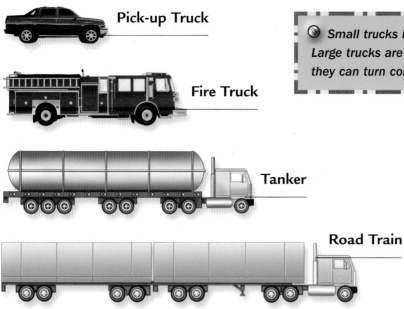

Pick-up Truck

Fire Truck

Tanker

Road Train

Small trucks have rigid bodies. Large trucks are articulated so that they can turn corners more easily.

FAST FACTS

Trailer Pick-up

To pick up a semi-trailer, a driver reverses the tractor unit underneath its front. A large pin on the trailer automatically slots into a hole on the tractor.

RIGID TRUCKS

Small trucks do not need to be articulated. They only need two front wheels, so they can go round corners without needing to bend in the middle. All rigid trucks have a rigid chassis with a cab for the driver at the front. Any sort of body, from a simple box for cargo to a complex cement mixer, can be built on the back.

The chassis of a rigid truck. It contains the engine, wheels and cab. It is ready for a body to be added.

Rear wheels
Turned by the engine

Air deflector
Deflects air over the body

Chassis
Made from strong steel

Small cab
Contains driving controls, but no sleeping compartment

HOW TRUCKS WORK

All trucks, big or small, work in a similar way. They have large wheels and tyres to carry heavy loads, a powerful engine, plenty of gears and air-powered brakes.

UNDER THE BONNET

There are two designs of truck cab – conventional and cabover. In a conventional truck the engine is in front of the cab under a long bonnet. In a cabover cab the engine is under the cab. This makes the cab shorter and gives more space behind for cargo.

🔩 *In a cabover truck, the whole cab tilts forwards so mechanics can service and repair the engine.*

Engine
Drives the truck

Gearbox
Connects the engine to the wheels

Fuel tank
Contains enough fuel to drive hundreds of kilometres

🔩 *A conventional truck. A shaft that turns the rear wheels goes under the cab.*

Scania Euro 3 Engine

Capacity	11 litres
Cylinders	in-line six
Power	380 hp
Gears	up to 14

Flywheel

Turbocharger

Piston inside cylinder

A diesel engine ready to be installed in a truck.

ENGINES AND GEARS

Almost all trucks are powered by a powerful diesel engine. A big engine has a capacity of 16 litres or more, giving plenty of power to pull 40,000 or 50,000 kilograms of cargo. Truck engines have turbochargers that pump air into the cylinders. This allows extra fuel to be burned for extra power. Trucks can have 18 or more gears — low ones for starting off and going uphill, and high ones for road cruising.

FAST FACTS
Mighty Engines

A truck engine is ten times as big as a family car engine and it has ten times the power. It weighs the same as the car, too!

A truck's driving wheels and suspension. A drive shaft from engine turns the wheels.

Brakes
Need to be powerful

Suspension
Spring lets wheels go up and down

Tyres
Spread weight of truck

7

EARLY TRUCKS

Before trucks were invented, more cargo was carried by boats and trains than on the roads. Things changed in the 1800s, when steam engines began to replace horses for pulling wagons.

Cargo
Carried on flat bed

Funnel
Carries away smoke and steam

> A steam truck built in England in the 1920s by the Foden company.

STEAM TRUCKS

The first trucks were built in the mid-1800s. They were powered by steam engines. In a steam engine burning coal heated water, which boiled to make steam. The steam was fed to cylinders and made pistons move in and out of them to turn the wheels. Diesel and petrol engines were invented in the 1890s, but steam trucks were still in use until the 1920s.

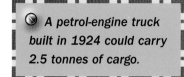
⊙ *A petrol-engine truck built in 1924 could carry 2.5 tonnes of cargo.*

Cab
With retractable roof

Petrol engine
In front of cab

Cylinder and piston
Drives the rear wheels round

Tipping body
Worked by hand

DIESEL DOMINATES

By the 1930s, trucks with petrol engines and diesel engines had taken over from trucks with steam engines. By the 1940s, however, most trucks were using diesel engines because they were cheaper to run than petrol engines.

⊙ *The Kenworth truck was designed to be able to lug a large quantity of cargo within economically constructed space.*

FAST FACTS
The First Truck
The first successful steam-powered vehicle was built in 1769 by a French military engineer named Nicolas Cugnot. It was designed to tow large guns.

9

CARGO TRUCKS

Truck bodies, semi-trailers and trailers are made in dozens of different shapes and sizes to carry all sorts of cargo.

TANKERS

Trucks with tanker bodies carry liquids such as oil, water and milk. The tank is in the shape of a cylinder, which makes it strong and also easy to make. Valves on top and at the rear are used for filling and emptying the tank. Bulk carriers are similar to tankers, but they carry powders such as cement and flour, instead.

Tank
Made from aluminium or steel

Hazard sign
Shows contents of tanker

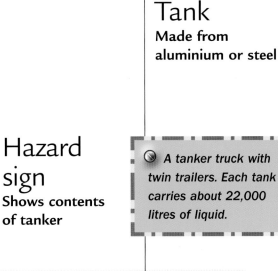
A tanker truck with twin trailers. Each tank carries about 22,000 litres of liquid.

○ A low-loader is a trailer that sits very close to the ground. It is designed to carry heavy vehicles such as diggers and tanks.

Low trailer
Allows vehicles to drive on and off

BODY STYLES

The most common truck bodies are flatbed bodies, box bodies, and bodies with flexible, removable sides (which are called curtain-siders). Flatbed bodies carry large loads that are lifted on and off by crane. Box bodies can be refrigerated, so they can carry cargo such as frozen foods. Cargo is tied down to stop it sliding about.

○ A tractor and box-body semi-trailer. The trailer's body has a simple frame covered with aluminium panels.

SPECIAL JOBS

Many types of truck don't carry cargo at all. Instead, their bodies have equipment mounted on them to do specialised jobs around towns, cities and airports.

UTILITY TRUCKS

Local authorities use several types of utility trucks. These are trucks built to do a special job. Refuse trucks move through the streets collecting rubbish from houses, factories, schools and shops. Road-sweeping trucks keep gutters clear, while snowploughs and grit spreaders keep roads safe when there is snow and ice.

Storage container

Sweeping mechanism

Body
Stores crushed rubbish

A refuse truck automatically lifts up bins, tips the rubbish into the truck, and crushes it into a small space.

Cab
For driver and crew

Bin
Tipped by mechanism

Blade
Spins to collect snow

This snowplough collects snow with a blade and blows it away to the roadside through a shoot.

AIRPORT TRUCKS

Busy airports have trucks that do lots of different jobs such as servicing aircraft and keeping the runways open. Refuelling tankers keep aircraft fuel tanks topped up. Aircraft tractors are the most specialised airport trucks. They push and pull heavy aircraft around the tarmac.

FAST FACTS
Always Ready

Airport fire trucks are always on stand-by when aircraft are taking off and landing, so they can attend to any emergency straightaway.

MIGHTY TRUCKS

An aircraft tractor sits close to the ground so that it can fit under the nose of an aircraft to hold onto the nose undercarriage.

SUPER MOVERS

Trucks are always on the move on construction sites. They move earth and rubble from place to place, and mix and pump concrete.

> A concrete mixer has a motor that turns the drum. It can carry several tonnes of concrete.

Chute
Unfolds to deliver concrete

Drum
Spins to mix concrete

CONCRETE MIXERS

A concrete mixing truck is a giant mixer on wheels. It starts its journey at a concrete factory where the ingredients of the concrete (cement, sand, gravel and water) are poured into its drum. At the building site the drum slowly turns round, mixing the ingredients together.

> A concrete pump is a truck that pumps fresh, runny concrete through pipes to where it is needed.

Boom

Delivery pipe

Stabilisers

14

TIPPER TRUCKS

Tipper trucks and dumper trucks move earth and rubble around building sites. They also work in quarries and mines. They have super-strong, open-topped bodies that are tipped up by hydraulic rams to pour their contents onto the ground. Tippers and dumpers have large wheels with chunky tyres to stop them sinking or slipping on muddy ground.

FAST FACTS

Concrete Carrier

A large concrete mixer can mix and carry as much as 15 bathtubs of concrete, weighing about 30,000 kilograms.

Cab
Contains controls for tipper

Hydraulic ram
Pushes body up to empty

Gate
Opens to let gravel pour out

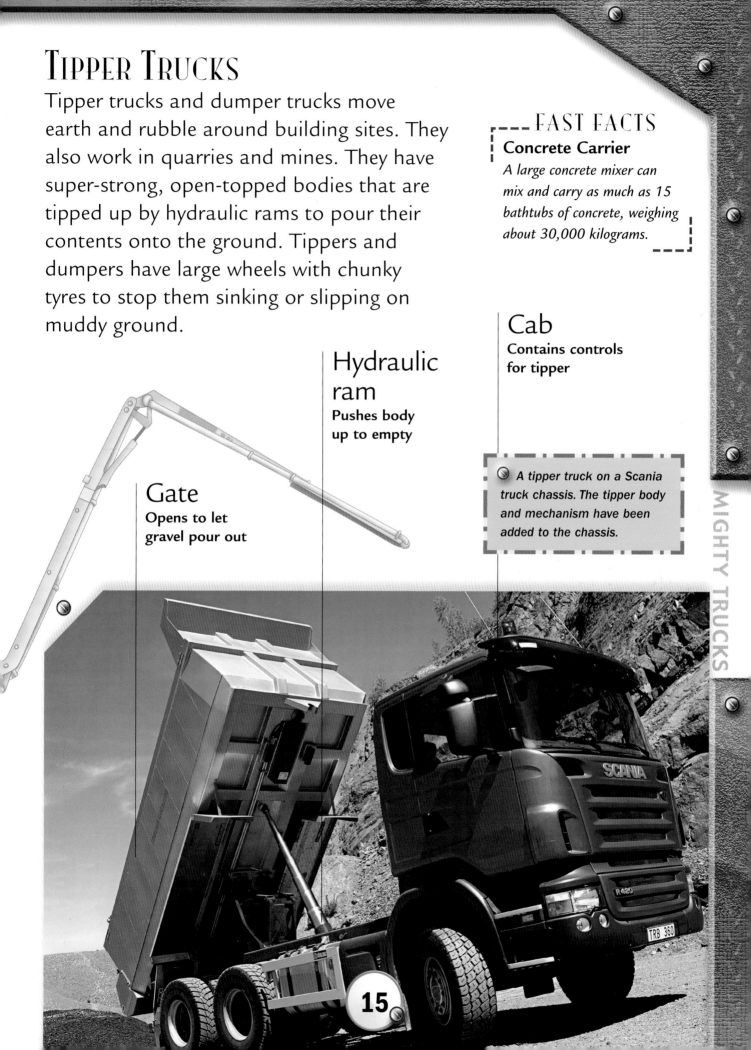

A tipper truck on a Scania truck chassis. The tipper body and mechanism have been added to the chassis.

15

MOBILE CRANES

A mobile crane is a crane mounted on top of a truck. The crane's arm folds away when the crane is driving along the road. It extends when the crane reaches the site.

MULTI-TERRAIN CRANE

The biggest mobile cranes are giant machines. Their crane arms are called booms and can reach high up into the air or extend far over the truck. These trucks are multi-terrain vehicles. They can cross bumpy, muddy building sites as well as drive on roads. Mobile cranes are used to lift and move exceptionally heavy loads, such as concrete beams for bridges.

Hydraulic ram
Lifts boom into the air

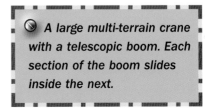

A large multi-terrain crane with a telescopic boom. Each section of the boom slides inside the next.

Crane boom
Folded away while on road

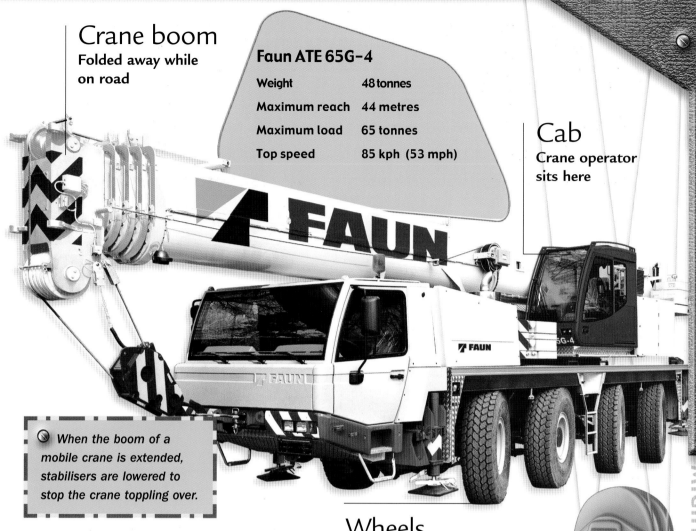

Faun ATE 65G-4

Weight	48 tonnes
Maximum reach	44 metres
Maximum load	65 tonnes
Top speed	85 kph (53 mph)

Cab
Crane operator sits here

When the boom of a mobile crane is extended, stabilisers are lowered to stop the crane toppling over.

Wheels
Each wheel has its own suspension

A flatbed truck loading building materials with the grappling tool on its on-board crane.

ON-BOARD CRANES

Many flatbed trucks have on-board cranes for loading and unloading cargo. The cranes lift materials from the truck onto the ground. These trucks are also called boom trucks.

FAST FACTS
Tallest Cranes
The biggest mobile cranes have booms that can reach more than 100 metres into the air. That's long enough to reach the 25th floor of an office block!

17

MILITARY TRUCKS

Armies use trucks for all sorts of things, such as transporting troops, equipment and supplies to the battlefield, and for helping in rescues after natural disasters.

The Oshkosh PLS off-road truck has a powered hook that loads and unloads equipment from its body.

Armoured front
Protects engine from rocks

Pallet
Changeable pallet for load

Wheels
All wheels are turned by the engine

Chunky tyres
Give grip in the mud

OFF-ROAD WORKERS

Military trucks often need to travel where other trucks can't go — along rough tracks and across fields, deserts and snow. To do this, the engine drives all the wheels round (this is called all-wheel drive). The wheels are large and the suspension is high. These features give lots of grip and space under the chassis for going over bumps.

A general-purpose military truck. It can tow trailers and guns as well as carry cargo.

FAST FACTS

Beach Landers

Amphibious vehicles are also used to land troops and equipment on beaches. They drive through the water from landing craft to the beach.

Radiator

Cools large, powerful diesel engine

AMPHIBIANS

Rivers are major obstacles for armies on the move. So, some army trucks are amphibious. This means they can drive on land like trucks, but they can also float in the water. Underneath, the chassis is sealed tight to stop water getting in.

Bison Amphibious Truck

Weight	11 tonnes
Engine	V8 supercharged diesel
Wheels	4 x 4
Maximum speed (land)	100 kph
Maximum speed (water)	10 kph (6.2 mph)

The Bison amphibious truck has inflatable floats to keep it stable in the water.

EMERGENCY!

Fire and rescue trucks are used by the emergency services to fight fires, rescue people trapped in cars and buildings, and recover vehicles.

Operator platform
for directing operations

Water pump

The Cobra 2 fire rescue vehicle has six-wheel drive, and water and foam tanks.

Equipment lockers

Cobra 2

Length	11.5 metres
Power	700 bhp
Water	10,000 litres
Foam	1,400 litres

FIRE TRUCKS

There are three main types of fire trucks – ladder trucks, water tenders and airport fire trucks. Ladder trucks have extending ladders that reach high into the air. Water tenders are general-purpose firefighting vehicles.

Large cab
With seats for crew

The ladder of a ladder truck extends to reach the upper floors of buildings. Firefighters work from the platform on the end of the ladder.

SUPERIOR TOWNSHIP FIRE DEPARTMENT

Lockers
For fire equipment

A rescue and recovery truck at the scene of an accident.

RECOVERY TRUCKS

A recovery truck is designed to rescue broken-down cars, buses and other trucks. Small recovery trucks can carry or tow a car. The biggest recovery trucks can tow double-decker buses and big trucks. They have powerful hooks that pick up the front of the broken-down vehicle to pull it along. They also have winches to pull vehicles from ditches.

FAST FACTS

Power Pumps

Fire trucks have powerful water pumps for spraying water. A typical pump can pour out 8,000 litres of water a minute. That's a bath-full every ten seconds!

A heavy-duty recovery truck for recovering broken-down and damaged trucks and buses.

CUSTOM TRUCKS

Truck enthusiasts like to customise their trucks. They add new parts to the truck bodies, make engines more powerful, and paint the bodies with interesting artwork.

CUSTOM PICK-UPS

Pick-up trucks are the smallest trucks. They are also the trucks that are most customised. Their owners add engine parts such as superchargers for extra power, wide wheels with big tyres, and high suspensions to lift the trucks high off the ground.

Customised pick-up trucks like this race in the NASCAR truck-racing series.

Roll cage
Protects driver in accident

Body shell
Aerodynamically shaped for speed

Cab
Leather seats can be added at the factory

The Ford F-150 pick-up truck can be customised by adding extra parts at the factory.

CUSTOM RIGS

'Rig' is the nickname for a truck or tractor unit. Some owners customise their rigs in the same way that pick-up owners do. They paint the cabs, add coloured lights and spotlamps and chrome parts, and keep the bodywork in perfect condition. Enthusiasts enter their trucks into competitions for the best custom rigs.

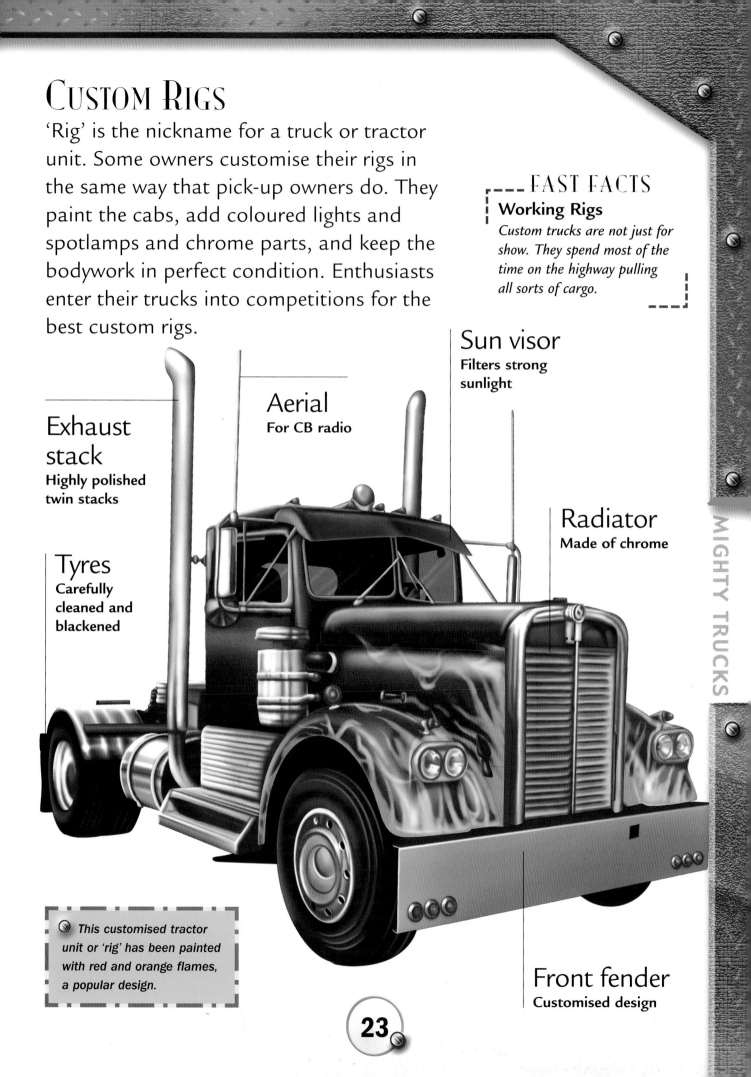

FAST FACTS
Working Rigs
Custom trucks are not just for show. They spend most of the time on the highway pulling all sorts of cargo.

Exhaust stack
Highly polished twin stacks

Aerial
For CB radio

Sun visor
Filters strong sunlight

Tyres
Carefully cleaned and blackened

Radiator
Made of chrome

This customised tractor unit or 'rig' has been painted with red and orange flames, a popular design.

Front fender
Customised design

TRUCK SPORT

Truck racing is a popular sport. Trucks race each other around race tracks and side by side around drag-racing tracks.

MONSTER TRUCKS

Monster trucks are amazing customised pick-up trucks with giant wheels and tyres normally used on dumper trucks. They also have super-powerful turbocharged engines and special suspensions that lift them high into the air. Monster trucks race each other around obstacle courses, jumping high over dirt ramps and piles of old squashed cars.

Bodywork
Painted and polished

> *Monster trucks always feature huge, outsized suspensions, wheels and tyres, a custom chassis and paintwork.*

High suspension
Lifts truck body above wheels

Dumper truck wheels and tyres
Let truck roll over giant obstacles

24

Truck racing is fast and furious. Trucks often collide as they try to overtake.

Engine
Standard engine with turbocharger

MAN Race Truck

Engine	6-cylinder turbo diesel
Power	1,050 hp
Weight	12.5 tonnes
Maximum speed	160 kph (100 mph)

TRUCKS ON TRACK

In another form of truck racing, the tractor units of articulated trucks are raced around tracks. There are local, national and international truck-racing championships. The trucks look like normal tractor units, with much more powerful engines, and features such as racing tyres, brakes and suspensions.

FAST FACTS
Truck vs Car
A racing tractor unit has an engine twenty times more powerful than a family car. It could leave the car standing in a race!

Drag-racing pick-up trucks race head-to-head on a short, straight track.

EXTREME TRUCKS

Here you can discover some of the world's heaviest trucks, longest trucks and most powerful trucks.

GIANT DUMP TRUCKS

The giants of the truck world are the mega dump trucks that work in quarries and open-cast mines. They carry huge loads of earth, rock and rubble. These monsters are the heaviest and tallest trucks. Their engines drive generators that produce electricity, which powers electric motors that drive the wheels.

Driver's cab
Reached by ladder from the ground

The Liebherr T 282B is the world's heaviest truck fully loaded.

Liebherr T 282B

Weight	320 tonnes
Power	3,618 hp
Maximum load	354 tonnes
Maximum speed	64 kph (40 mph)

Dumper
Tips up to dump load

Tyres
Each tyre taller than an adult

LIEBHERR

T 282B

140

Semi-trailers

Sleeper cab

A tanker road train being pulled by a super-powerful tractor.

MIGHTY TRUCKS

Giant loads are pulled on trailers with dozens of wheels by super-powerful heavy-haulage tractors.

ROAD TRAINS

Trucks often pull a trailer behind them, attached by a tow bar. A truck with two or more trailers is called a road train because it is like a railway locomotive that pulls lots of wagons. Road trains are popular in the Australian outback, where trucks travel with sheep, cattle and other cargo.

Load
Bolted firmly to truck

Tractor unit
Stays in low gear to pull load

27

FUTURE TRUCKS

In the future trucks will become even more efficient, using less fuel and making less pollution. They will use new technology, but will probably not look much different from the trucks of today.

All-glass cab
For good visibility

CONCEPT TRUCKS

A concept truck is an example of what truck manufacturers think their trucks might look like in a few years' time. Concept trucks feature interesting streamlined body shapes and new technologies that might be used in the future. Concept trucks are used to demonstrate new ideas.

Bumper
Collapses safely in accident

Air deflector
For fuel economy

Video cameras
For all-round vision when turning and reversing

Low-resistance tyres
For fuel economy

The Mitsubishi FUSO concept truck is designed to be safe for the driver and pedestrians, comfortable to drive, and environmentally friendly.

> A General Motors military truck. It has a diesel engine and a fuel cell for power.

Aerials
For radio communications

Cargo area
For troops and equipment

SELF-DRIVE TRUCKS

Some manufacturers are experimenting with autonomous trucks. An autonomous vehicle is a vehicle that drives itself so it doesn't need a human driver. It is remotely controlled by radio or is completely automatic. Autonomous trucks could be especially useful for armies. Then human drivers would not have to drive into dangerous situations.

FAST FACTS
Satellite Navigation
Autonomous trucks use the global positioning system (GPS) to find their way around the countryside.

> A Terramax all-terrain autonomous military truck. There is no driver!

TIMELINE

1769

French engineer Nicolas Cugnot builds a steam tractor for pulling military guns, creating the world's first powered vehicle.

1802

In England, Richard Trevithick builds a steam carriage that travels on the roads.

1804

The world's first amphibious vehicle is built in the USA.

1831

The British government brings in laws to stop steam-powered vehicles using the public roads because of safety fears.

1860

Frenchman Etienne Lenoir builds the first internal combustion engine.

1876

The first truck, a steam-powered machine weighing 4 tonnes (3.9 tons), is built in England.

1885

In Germany, Karl Benz builds the first motor car, using a gas-powered internal combustion engine.

1885

Gottlieb Daimler builds the first petrol-powered internal combustion engine.

1896

Daimler builds the first petrol-powered truck.

1897

German engineer Rudolf Diesel demonstrates his diesel engine.

1898

The first articulated truck is made by the Thornycroft company.

1904

Power steering is introduced in trucks.

1907

The first truck show is held in Chicago, USA.

1914

The first truck production line is started by the Ford company in the USA.

1914–18

Trucks transport troops and equipment in World War I.

1920s

The cabover engine layout is developed, trucks begin using pneumatic tyres, and the first six-wheel rigid trucks are built.

1930s

Manufacturers experiment with streamlined trucks.

1950s

Diesel engines become widely used in trucks.

1954

Volvo introduces turbocharged diesel engines.

2003

The world's longest road train is put together in Australia.

GLOSSARY

amphibious

A truck that can work as a boat as well as move on land.

articulated truck

A truck made up of a tractor unit and a semi-trailer, with a flexible joint between them.

cabover

A tractor unit or rigid truck with the cab over the top of the engine.

chassis

The solid frame of a tractor unit or rigid truck.

cylinder

A space inside an engine that a piston moves in and out of. Burning fuel or high-pressure steam pushes the piston out, making the engine work.

diesel engine

An internal combustion engine that uses diesel fuel and does not have spark plugs like a petrol engine.

hydraulic

Describes a machine that has parts operated by liquid pushed along pipes.

internal combustion engine

An engine in which the fuel is burned inside the cylinders. Petrol and diesel engines are internal combustion engines.

petrol engine

An internal combustion engine that uses petrol as fuel, which is ignited by electric spark plugs in the cylinders.

pneumatic tyre

A tyre that is filled with air. All modern vehicles have pneumatic tyres, but the first trucks had solid rubber tyres.

power steering

A steering system that uses some power from a truck's engine to make turning the steering wheel easier.

rigid truck

A truck with a single rigid chassis, with the cab and body built on top.

road train

A truck made up of a tractor unit or rigid truck with two or more trailers towed behind.

streamlined

With a smooth shape that moves easily through the air.

supercharger

A device that pumps air into an engine, allowing more fuel to be burned, and thereby improving power.

suspension

A system of springs and dampers that allow a truck's wheels to move up and down over bumps in the ground.

tractor

The front part of an articulated truck, containing the engine, cab and driving wheels.

turbocharger

A device that pumps air into an engine, allowing more fuel to be burnt and thus improving power. It is powered by exhaust gases.

INDEX

WEBFINDER

http://www.worldfiretrucks.com *Hundreds of photographs of fire trucks.*

http://www.oshkoshtruck.com *Home page of Oshkosh trucks.*

http://trucktrend.com *Features on all types of truck, past, present and future.*

http://www.liebherr.com/lh/en/ *Information on trucks and cranes, including the world's heaviest truck.*

http://www.monstertruckracing.com *Photographs and information on monster truck racing.*

http://www.faun.de/index-e.htm *Website of Faun mobile cranes.*

http://www.macktrucks.com *Official site of Mack, a giant American truck builder.*

http://www.roadtrains.com.au *Site dedicated to giant road trains. Lots of photographs.*